THIS
BOOK
BELONGS TO:

_____

Typical clock from the Black Forest

Cherries for the Black Forest Cake

Traditional headgear for women in the Black Forest

Squirrel in the Black Forest

Black Forest Cake

A cow in the Black Forest

On top of mountain Kandel

Pine cone in the Black Forest

Pretzel

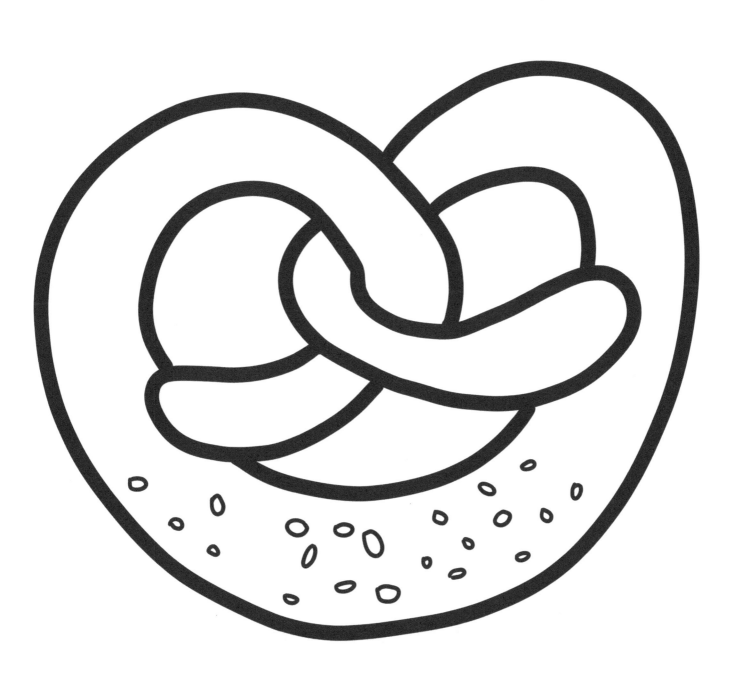

Traditional house in the Black Forest

Hirschsprung (deer jump) in Höllental

Traditional straw shoes

Mountain railway to mountain Schauinsland

Typical soup (broth with pancake stripes) called Flädlesuppe

Typical Lacquer Shield Clock

Pinetree in the Black Forest

Carnival in the Black Forest – here you see a costume called Rägemolli typical for a town called Elzach

Tower on top of Feldberg mountain

Paragliding

Hiking with boots in the Black Forest

Traditional Black Forest costume

Top of cathedral tower in Freiburg

Black Forest ham

Biggest Advent Calendar House of the world
in a town called Gengenbach

Bridge over Ravenna Gorge

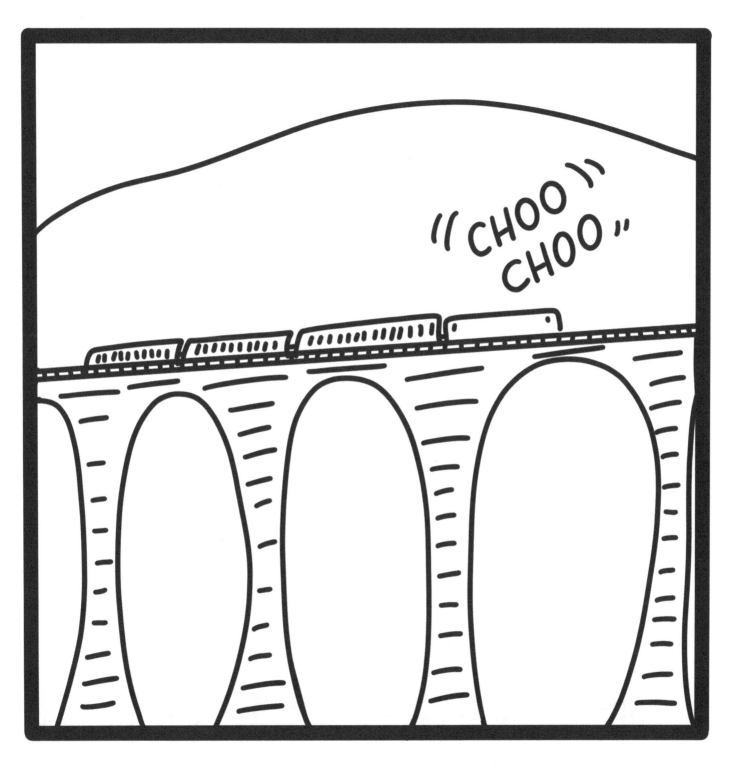

Hexenloch Mill
(literally translates as witch's hole mill)

Saint Peter Convent
in a town called Sankt Peter

Boat tour on lake Schluchsee

Black Forest bread from a wood fired oven

Cross on top of Belchen mountain

CONGRATULATIONS

Wow, you did it! You colored in 30 different motifs from the Black Forest. You now deserve this Black Forest Certificate! Write your name below and cut it out afterwards.

BLACK FOREST CERTIFICATE

Write your name here

got to know 30 different aspects of the Black Forest.

Hereby the Black Forest Certificate is awarded.

Can be cut out here

Made in United States
Cleveland, OH
30 November 2024